Sheffi

and Folklore since the Second World War: a Dying Tradition

Second Edition

David Battye

© David Battye 2009

Cartoons: Mychailo Kazybrid

Printed and published by:
ALD Design & Print
279 Sharrow Vale Road
Sheffield S11 8ZF

Telephone 0114 267 9402
E:mail a.lofthouse@btinternet.com

ISBN 9781901587678

First published October 2007, Second Edition June 2009

Sheffield Dialect
and Folklore since the Second World War: a Dying Tradition

Second Edition

David Battye

New enlarged edition

It was inevitable that my memory would let me down and allow me to forget many words, phrases etc. I am pleased to say that many people have willingly reminded me of the items I had forgotten and these are now included in what I hope is the complete version of Sheffield usage and practices at the end of the 20th Century. Additionally, I have recovered yet more words from the hidden depths of my memory.

Perhaps the silliest omission was 'shunkly', how I came to forget this I cannot imagine. I just plead old age, and leave it at that. I have taken the opportunity to amend some of the previous entries, and also to cut one out that I got all wrong.

I am grateful to those many fellow citizens who have informed me of the several omissions and some corrections. Many of these were presented to me unwittingly as I heard casual conversations on the street, in shops and on the tram, the Sheffield way of speech is alive and well! I hope that these several amendments are enjoyed and again I commend the dialect of this wonderful city in which I have lived all my life.

The dialect of the Sheffield area has developed over many years and shows the several influences of those who have lived in the town. Sheffield is shaped and controlled by its geography. Its position in the foothills of the Pennines should have ensured that it stayed as little more than a small market town. Had it not been for the development of its many natural resources, there is almost a certainty that this would have happened.

As things turned out, this was not to be. The development of first water resources, then coal to create the power for the metal and engineering industries provided the driving force to overcome the geographical problems and create what is now Britain's fourth largest city.

This growth was achieved by absorbing people from many sources and some of these have left their mark on the dialect words of the area. Indeed the words themselves indicate a wide variety of origins, stretching back to the Viking invasions of the Dark

1

Ages. These have been further modified by local speech patterns and pronunciations which I have tried to present in this account.

This book is a list of words and phrases which I have heard used in Sheffield in my lifetime, essentially since the Second World War, I was born in 1939. Some I have not heard for many years but still remember them clearly. Most I have had to guess at a spelling, I hope that it agrees with other people's opinion.

Dialect is a variation of a language still with most of the main elements of that language being used. Much of what is sold commercially as examples of Sheffield dialect is nothing of the sort, merely slipshod speech. Missing aitches and other missing letters, slurred words and unclear enunciation are not confined to Sheffield or any other part of the country. What is often sold as `Sheffield` (or, even worse, `Shevveld`) are just examples of careless speech.

An example is the old saying `Oo washee wi', washee wi' er sen?` (Who was she with ,was she alone?) This is frequently presented as Sheffield dialect to perplex the outsider. However, oo is just a missing aitch sound from who, washee is just a slovenly was of saying 'was she', wi' is a form of with which could be met in most parts of the kingdom. The only Sheffield dialect form is 'hersen', meaning herself. Because of this I have tried not to include examples of slipshod speech in my list except as illustrative examples of the use of the dialect.

I have omitted trade words. All trades have their own peculiar words and expressions, the cutlery, steelmaking and other trades around Sheffield are no exception, but they are not words which were in general use. The same can be said of farming and rural trades; in general their specialised expressions have not been included in the list.

Many readers will notice that some words or phrases with which they are familiar have been omitted. This is due to the list being limited to my own memory. Equally, there will be examples where readers are mystified by the inclusion of examples they have never heard of, please accept that I have heard these used in the time span I am using, since the second world war. I am sure that I have also included words or phrases with a far wider currency than just Sheffield and South Yorkshire, where this has happened please accept that I have always regarded them as local in origin, probably wrongly.

Throughout the list it is assumed that the reader will be familiar with local pronunciation. The accent is similar to other West Riding accents with short `a`, hard `u` and other Northern vowel sounds. Sheffielders are adept at turning any vowel sound into at least a diphthong. I have selected t' as the method I will use to represent the Northern `the`, frankly I do not believe that we have a suitable way of showing this in our alphabet.

I have also, to record them, included some examples of playground lore and games from my childhood and also local customs. Many of the usages in the list have already become obsolete and there is no doubt that others will follow them into history very soon. The influences of national media and a more mobile population are contributors to this increasing tendency. Recently it has been revealed that the influence of mobile phones, e-mail and the internet are accelerating the decline of local usage. Accents still remain, dialect and folklore are becoming harmonised into the standard national model.

It is for the reasons in the previous paragraph that I want to set down the position as it was when I was a child in the 1940s and 50s, to preserve a record before even more is lost to memory.

This is an affectionate tribute to a past way of speech of which much has already gone and more will follow. I hope that you will enjoy happy memories if you shared the experiences with me, or that you will find interest if you are new to the wonders of mid 20th century Sheffield.

A Often used instead of 'on' to denote a day of the week. "Ah bowt some fish a Monday an' nah its gone reight off."

Ackermatoota (Some of the old glossaries present it as `ackermantut`, I have never heard this used in speech). A gardeners' concoction created, usually, by collecting a sack full of sheep manure, tying it tightly and immersing the sack in a water butt. (Most of the water butts were the old galvanised washing tubs with ribbed sides). The water is then used as liquid manure, most especially on greenhouse grown tomatoes. The `acker` part of the name obviously comes from the Latin 'aqua' meaning water. The rest I have no idea about. I remember gathering the manure and creating the material as late as the 1960s. It did smell awful, but was supposed to be wonderful for tomatoes!

Addle Has the wide Yorkshire dialect meaning of 'to earn'. Thus a person will 'addle their brass', that is 'work for their money'.

All reight? (often pronounced `orreight?`)A general greeting to which only a positive response is acceptable. The normal reply is something like, "Aye, I'm all reight, are tha?" Many will remember a similar reply in "The Full Monty" when the respondent was in no way all right but was stranded on a car roof in the middle of the canal.

And all (never pronounced like this, but always `an all`) As well. "Ah went to pictures an' ahr kid come an' all".

Anyroad Anyway. "Ah know it's rainin' but ah'm gooin' to t'football match anyroad."

Article Chamber pot. When I first heard this ridiculous euphemism, I thought that it was peculiar to one family, but I then heard it used by another, quite unrelated so far as I could see. It carries on a long tradition of never referring to 'unseemly' items directly, but always via some seemingly innocuous word. This has provided 'guzzunda' and 'potty' and 'po' for the chamber pot, as well as this quite meaningless example. (see 'nessy').

Ar Common pronunciation of 'Aye' meaning `yes`. "Asta fun thi cat?" "Ar, we 'ave."

Arse Not now used in polite society, but widely still in use. GHB Ward recounted many local stories in the 'Clarion Rambler' books. He tells of a Methodist Local Preacher in the mid 19th century telling a congregation, "I'd as soon see a pig run arse'ards up a tree and whistle like a throstle as see a rich man enter t'kingdom of 'eaven."

Arundel (as in the name of local roads etc.) Usually pronounced with the stress on the second syllable, Arundel as distinct from the pronunciation of the castle/town in Sussex with that name, where the stress is on the first syllable, Arundel.

Ass 'Ash' as in the dust at the bottom of a fire. It is more widely met with joined to other words, such as 'asscan' or 'asspit'.

Asta? This is the first example of the still widespread usage of thee, thy and thou instead of you and your. In many parts of the North the use of `thee` and `thou` is still common, Sheffield is no exception. Asta is a blend of two words into one, `Hast thou?' or 'Have you?' "Asta bin to t' market today?"

Aye `Yes`. Still very widely used in the district, as often pronounced 'Ar'.

Babby Common pronunciation of 'baby'. A schoolgirl commenting on the holocaust said with horror, "Tha meeans they did it to babbies an' all?"

Back end Autumn. There appears never to have been an equivalent `front end` meaning spring.

Backus Bake house.

Badly Sick, as in "How are tha feeling, Tom?" "I'm reight badly, lad."

Baht Another Yorkshire dialect usage, meaning without. Nowadays more familiar in the county's national anthem, "On Ilkley Moor baht 'at" (On Ilkley Moor without a hat, hence the illness and death in the song). In some versions of "Ilkley Moor" the words are presented as 'bah tat' which is absolute nonsense. The story is told of a Yorkshire soldier on parade and being told off by the sergeant for not having a rifle. "Where's your rifle, man?" "I aven't bin gen wun," he replied. The sergeant turned to another man whom he knew came also from Yorkshire, "What is this man saying?" he asked. "He's baht," was the answer.

7

Bank Holiday Tuesday There is really no such thing, but Sheffield has managed to invent it, especially at Easter. Hot metal industries take time to get back into production after a shutdown so, in the days when most worked Saturday mornings, the city ignored Good Friday as a day off (except for the banks) and took the day following Easter Monday. This established the pattern. Good Friday gradually became widely used as a holiday only over the last thirty or so years.

Bass (male singing voice) pronounced as the name of the beer with a short `a`. Since I am one and occasionally drink the other I quite approve of this.

Beast Cattle used for beef production. Butchers in Sheffield sell offal, as do all butchers. This would include lambs' kidneys, pigs' kidneys and beasts' kidneys. The word is still in use in this form, often pronounced `beeast`. Beast cheek was widely used for brawn.

Beauchief The name of the suburb is pronounced Beechiff. Sheffielders have no more respect for the French language than anywhere else in the UK.

Beaumont This is the name of several roads in the Manor Park area and the name is pronounced 'Bewmont'. I taught for several years at Waltheof School which is on 'Bewmont Close'.

Beck A general Northern usage to describe a small stream. At the top of Bradfield Dale is Agden Beck.

Bee-byes Baby talk meaning sleep as in "Go to bee-byes, darling".

Beers Sheffield used to have several large breweries with some locally produced beers that were well known over a large area. Two of these had very particular pronunciations. Stones was pronounced `Stooanses` and Wards `Waards` with the middle part sounding like `are`.

Strangely, Wards was never pronounced `Wardses`, which would be logical, following `Stooanses`.

Beer Off Off-licensed shop. The licensing laws offer two major types of licence, an `on-licence` whereby the seller is able to sell alcoholic drink for consumption on the premises, such as a pub, and an `off-licence` whereby any drink sold must be taken away. Further, there are separate licences available for beer and for wines & spirits. In most parts of Sheffield the idea of buying whole bottles of wine or spirits was rare and many shops had beer licences only, hence the name `beer off`. Up to the late 1940s it was not uncommon for this beer to be collected in jugs and many beer offs had hand pumps for this purpose. The beer was often collected by a child and the placing of a cloth over the top of the jug was probably a way of suggesting that the child would never ever taste the beer, as if!

Belly wark Stomach ache. `Wark` can be attached to any useful word such as `Ear wark`, `'Eead wark` etc., but recently I have only heard it referring to the stomach. "Ah went to t' doctor cus ah had belly wark".

Be nah `By now`. "'E must have got hooam be nah, sithee, t' bus's gooin' back to town."

Bent grass Rough moorland grass, mainly met in place names such as Bent's Green. Sometimes just used as a place name 'Bents'.

Berrited; buried. "She wor berrited at Wisewood cimmetreh".

Berryin cake (=Burying cake) Seed cake with caraway seeds in. It must have been such a common sight at funeral teas that the name has stuck. I first remember having it at a favourite uncle's funeral and have had a liking for it ever since.

Besom A condemnatory term used for another person. I have mainly heard it of a woman. In most of the dialect books it seems to mean a loose woman, I have only heard it used in Sheffield as describing a stroppy, awkward girl or woman. "She's a reight besom". Sometimes the word is used affectionately when applied to a child.

Bilk Fail to pay a debt.

Bill's mother's Is responsible for much of the city's bad weather. "It is looking black o'er Bill's mother's" refers to oncoming bad weather. When I was a child I was puzzled by the phrase because it was applied to dark clouds in any direction from the house, I could not believe that Bill's mother could live in so many different places.

Billyo Fast, in the sense of rapid. "He's goin' like billyo."

Biting on Snack taken between meals. "I allus give 'im a bitin' on when he gets home from schoil". This would keep him going to tea time.

Black clock Black beetle, usually the ground beetle.

Bobbaa Sorry about this, my brother told me that I had to include it for completion (he would!, but he was right). It was a childish name for excrement (and that's a very polite way of putting it!) I haven't heard it for years. I have included several childish names in this list. They are, of course, adult names really, used to address children. I can never understand the need for them. It can only be confusing to a child to have to learn a new name at a later age, rather than use the proper one from the start.

Bobby dazzler something, usually a person, decked out in all its finery. "Tha looks a reight bobby dazzler in thi new suit."

Bobby's job Any job that does not involve hard physical labour. Working men at the beginning of the last century would rarely meet, in any social sense, people who had white collar type jobs. Police were recruited from all levels of society and the sons of manual workers would be thought to have entered a really easy life if the became a bobby, hence 'Bobby's job'. "Ahr Jim's got a reight bobby's job, drivin' t'gaffer abaht in 'is car."

11

Bonny Euphemism for fat, in the sense of overweight. A bonny woman does not mean the same as it would in more northerly areas when it would refer to general attractiveness. In Sheffield it is generally applied to a fat woman or child, I have never heard it used of a man. I find its use a kindly one, bonny being probably regarded as a preferable word to use. "Tha knows Mrs Walker, she's t'bonny woman dahn't rooad."

Boook Common local pronunciation of `book` to produce the same `oo` sound as in `doom`. I have hard the same being done with `look`, `cook` and `hook`, but far less often (see `cuke`).

Borrow A loan. "Can ah `ave a borrer of thi pencil?" (see lend for the same usage).

Botch Local usage of the word `bodge`. A job which has not been properly carried out is `botched`.

Bottom Used to describe a valley floor. An example would be `Loxley Bottom` referring to the stretch of the valley from Wisewood to Bradfield. More often used in the plural as `Loxley Bottoms`.

Bottom A verbal use meaning to really deal with the whole job, especially on cleaning. "She come 'ooam and set to cleanin' t' whole house an' really bottomin' it".

Brad Small headless nail. I realise that this word has widespread use over the whole country, but I have included it because it was in the Glossary of the Sheffield Dialect produced in 1888 by the English Dialect Society. This book was very useful as a prompt to my memory. I suspect that the compilers of that book were rather middle class and probably had never met a brad in their lives, hence they believed that it was a local dialect word.

Brass Common Yorkshire use as meaning `money`. Hence, "Where there's muck there's brass."

Brat Apron, usually worn by a workman in such places as a warehouse, butcher's or grocer's.

Brawnge To boast. Can also become a noun as in, "He were allus a reight brawnger even when he hadn't nowt to brawnge abaht".

Bread and cheese The young leaves of the hawthorn. They are eatable and when I was a child my mother persuaded me to do so, saying that this was called bread and cheese. I must say that although they had no nasty taste, they certainly did not taste of bread and cheese. I tested this recently and tried them again, still no result.

Breadcake Sheffield does not use the word `bun` for a small bread product and, except when called it an 'oven bottom cake' will always use `breadcake`, usually expressed as a single word. Roll is a rather posh recent usage in the town. I do not remember hearing the word 'bap' until well after the war, possibly in the 1960s. Breadcakes are plain, as distinct from teacakes which have currants of raisins in. I understand that in Stocksbridge this is not so and they are called, plain and fruited teacakes.

Brick Used for any small stone. When I was at primary school I remember us having a `brick feight` with a local group of boys. For all the suggestion of violence it was actually safer than a `fist feight`. In the second it was certain that someone would be hurt, usually with a bleeding nose at least. In the `brick feight` it was normal to dodge all the bricks and yet still feel that satisfaction was assured.

Brickle Brittle, this is not a slovenly use of the word, it comes from Old English `brokel`.

Brock Broken. "A bloke's bike's back brake block brock" has been used as a local tongue twister.

Broddle To poke around. The last time I heard it was of someone `broddling` in his ear.

Brussen Burst, probably now no longer used. We was all sent ooam cus t' boiler were brussen."

Brussen Brazen, in the sense of uppity or cheeky. "She were a brussen little beggar". Most words referring to the stroppiness of children seem to have mainly been applied to girls. Girls were 'brussen' or 'besoms'. Boys were 'just lads'. Make of this what you will!

Buffet (The final letter is pronounced) This is a small footstool, usually padded. It is probably a local attempt to pronounce the French word `pouffee`, now a normal English word. "Sit thisen down on yon buffet lad and shut up". See also `tuffet`.

Bull week Last of the trio of weeks leading to Christmas when the workers in the cutlery industry tried to increase their output to provide for a good feast. The third week before was `calf week`, then `cow week` and finally `bull week`. In Wadsley, where I live, the candle ends were collected over the year and when the little mester completed his allocation of work in bull week, the ends were all arranged on the window sills and lit,

Bunfire Still widely used pronunciation of bonfire.

By..... An introduction to the various names of 'deities' by which the Sheffield residents would swear an oath. Not that the present day users would either consider it to be an oath, nor that they would consider the subjects to be deities. The common Yorkshire phrase 'by gum' is used, but rather infrequently, 'by 'eck' less rarely, perhaps it is more usual to say 'by ...' with a definite break after it. . "By ..., but thart a lucky lad. Ah nivver 'ad a bike at thy age."

Cabbaging Trying to gain an unfair advantage by creeping forwards in a game. Could be a footballer taking a throw much nearer the opposition goal than he should, could be a marble player creeping forward to make the shot shorter. Was always regarded as a serious infringement. "Gi'o'er cabbaging, tha cheeatin' devil".

Cack handed Clumsy. "He were a reight cack handed beggar". Also used for left handedness. In my recollection there were no other terms used in my part of Sheffield for left handedness. I suppose that the two uses together are rather derogatory to those who are left handed, my father was one and he was no more clumsy than the rest of us.

Calf licked Having a mop of hair where there is an uncontrollable tuft above the eye where 'a calf has licked it'. The mop of hair was sometimes called a 'calf lick'.

Calf week See Bull week.

Carol Singing in the north of the city is a well defined ritual. It begins the week after Remembrance Day and proceeds to Christmas. The carols are sung in a series of local pubs, each with their defined place on the calendar. The carols sung are mainly peculiar to the area in which they are sung, although this area extends well into more northern parts of the West Riding. The events attract a large crowd of enthusiastic supporters. Many of the carols and their tunes were collected and written down by a vicar of Stannington around the beginning of the last century. A great uncle of mine, a Goddard, published these for sale, and they were very popular. He was successfully sued for breach of the vicar's copyright by the man's descendants. I do not think that losing the suit placed any brake on his sales, from his music shop in Middlewood Road, and in the 1940's and 50's they were well known as 'Goddard's carols'.

Cater cornered (Sometimes pronounced `catey corner`) placed aslant rather than at right angles. Especially applied to a house which is at the junction of a road and not in line with either road but place at an angle in the corner. I was born in a cater cornered house on Swanbourne Road.

Causey Causeway, all recent uses I have heard have been of `causey edge` (that is the kerb).

Chance what No matter what happens. "Chance what, you can bet that our 'Arry 'll come up smellin'o' roses".

Chara Still used as an abbreviation for `charabanc`, the old style 1920`s coach where the seats were in rows raised higher and higher towards the back of the bus, in French the chairs were in a bank or `char-a-banc`. When used in full, which is rarely, it is pronounced `Charabang`. Children at schools are still often likely to say, when going on a school trip, "Miss, when's t'chara coming?"

Chavel To tear away in small pieces. A paving stone can become chavelled at the edges.

Chimbley Chimney.

Chin cough Whooping cough. "If tha sits on t'floor tha'll get chin cough".

Chitterlings The entrails of an animal sold to be fried as a meal. Not just a Sheffield word, but certainly a dying (even dead?) food. When I worked for a butcher they were always pig intestines and were sold along with the stomach as `chitterlings and bag`. We always had a regular clientele, especially because they were off the ration. I could never bring myself to eat them, or even think of eating them.

Chizzler Swindler. Chizzle can also be used, meaning to cheat.

Chock A wedge shaped piece of wood used to prop

open a door or to prevent a wheeled vehicle from running away. In the 1940s a chock was carried on all Sheffield buses to enable them to be secured when they failed or were parked on the many steep hills.

Chock full Totally full, "T' box were chock full of rubbish".

Chomp Chew, or perhaps rather to use the teeth to crush whatever is in the mouth. Used perhaps more of brittle food such as mint rock or biscuits. "Ah can eear thee chompin' thi spice from 'ere." Chomping almost always seemed to be carried out with the mouth open.

Choose how Any how. "I will go to town on t' bus, choose how".

Chow To chew (food).

Chrysants (sometimes Chrisses) Chrysanthemums. For most of my lifetime, and still for many gardeners and allotment holders, the pinnacle of Autumn gardening has been the production of fabulously large Chrysants. You still often see proud growers carrying bunches of them home.

Chuck Hen.

Chuck Throw, also to break off a relationship, " She's chucked 'im and is gooin' wi' Jack". "'Ee chucked a brick through me mam's window."

Chuffed Delighted. "I am chuffed with our new car" (Perhaps more usually "I am dead chuffed….")

Chunter Grumble.

Cimmetry Cemetery.

Clack Chatter. `Shut thi clack, tha'rt mekkin' me ill'.

Clack was also used to describe the small fleshy lump hanging down at the back of the mouth, the epiglottis.

Claggy Sticky, such as clay or a rather `fallen` pudding.

Clart To cover with too much butter, or jam or similar. 'Tha's clarted t' bread wi' butter ageean, does ta think I'm made o' brass?'

Clarty Sticky, such as when hands have jam or honey on them. "Ah dooant like 'oney cos it meks me 'ands all clarty."

Clemmed I can only ever remember hearing this being used once in the Sheffield area. It is a common Yorkshire dialect word and means hungry.

Clever beggar A show off. "'E's a reight clever beggar

sin' 'e passed t' scholarship"

Clock Seed head of a dandelion. A common children's belief was that you could tell the time by seeing how many puffs were needed to blow away all the seeds. One puff equals one hour. I do not think children ever really believe this, they just like doing it.

Clock Common beetle. Usually the black ground beetle, called a `black clock`.

Clock To hit somebody as punishment. "Clock him one, t' cheeky begger".

Clock Cold Completely cold when it should have been warm, usually of food or drink. "T' tea what she poured me were clock cowd".

Close Tight fisted, mean, usually only applied to someone who is at least reasonably well off. There does seem to be rather a lot of words for meanness in this list. I suppose it was the absolute pinnacle of bad neighbourliness in the days of low incomes and before the welfare state.

Clout Cloth. The same as in the saying, `Ne'er cast a clout until May is out`. Particularly used of 'dish clout'.

Cob nut Horse chestnut fruit, conker.

Cobs When exercising heavily one sweats cobs. I am not sure what cobs are, but I have often sweated them. Only recently a man on the tram said to the world in general, "I've rushed all t' way from Coles an' ahm sweatin' cobs". We all knew what he was talking about.

Cockle To become bent or wrinkled, to fall over on a rough surface. 'This newspaper's all cockled up at t' corners.' 'T' bottle of milk cockled ovver and spilt.'

Cockloft The attic of a house, also the area under the eaves. This is the place where Christmas ornaments and holiday cases are stored.

Cod Pod, usually of a pea, "Pea cod".

Coil Coal, as in "Coil `ole", coal cellar.

Collyfobble Cheat. Used in a variety of ways. 'I couldn't get t' knife blade to fit, but I managed to collyfobble it on.' 'She wor playin' cards an' she collyfobbled 'er way to win.'

Collywobbles Butterflies in the stomach, nervousness. "Asta met Mester Smith, t' new teacher? 'Ee gives me collywobbles."

Conk Nose (of a person).

Cop Catch. This is used not just of catching such as by a policeman (hence "copper") but also, for example, to "cop a cold".

Cornish Mantlepiece. Undoubtedly a corruption of `corniche`, the French word for a ledge.

Cow week Two weeks before Christmas, followed by Bull Week and preceded by Calf Week. (See Bull week).

Cowd Cold. (It is rather difficult to accurately represent the pronunciation of this word, probably more like `cowed` to rhyme with 'owed', some speakers manage to insert an 'e' between the 'c' and the 'o').

Cowk Core (of an apple) (see Us below). Also met in the expression 'grindle cowk', meaning a worn down grind stone, that is the core of a grind stone. These were often used for a variety of purposes, stepping stones, door/gate stops and so on,

Cranky Bad tempered.

Crinkle To become creased as in "Keep still, thart crinkling t' sheets".

Cross hobbled The mismatching of buttons and buttonholes. "Tha's got thi jacket all cross hobbled ageean, come 'ere an' let me sort thee out." It must take its origin from the practice of hobbling farm animals for transport, or to stop straying, by tying a rope from the fore foot on one side to the rear on the other which was very ungainly.

Crozzle To cook very well, meat can be `crozzled` and is nearly burned, but not quite. A lot of food tastes better when its crozzled.

Cuckoo spit The froth on a plant in Summer produced by the froghopper.

Cuke Pronunciation of `cook`. A woman who lives near us pronounced the word `cook` to rhyme with `Nuke`. She once criticised my mother for working saying, "I 'ave no time for workin', I spend all my time cukink".

Cumber Cucumber.

Cut Canal, any man made watercourse.

Cutlery (often pronounced 'cucklery') Refers to knives only. Forks and spoons are flatware or hollow ware.

Cuttle To make knives, in other words to be a cutler.

Dadle Dawdle.

Dannies Childish name for hands.

Dateless Silly, a description of somebody who has no idea even of what day it is.

Daystone Rock lying naturally on the surface of the ground and large enough to be used in building. Many such rocks lie around the `edges` above the Sheffield valleys and were used as easy quarrying material. Very large daystones were broken up on site and then used as quarried material.

Dee To die.

Dee, also **Da** Meaning thee or thou. Sheffielders habitually used `d` instead of `th` at the beginning of words. In the first world war the members of (especially) the York & Lancaster Regiment, recruiting strongly in the city, were known by other troops as the "Dee Dahs". Far less common recently and has tended to be replaced by 'thee' and 'tha'.

A Sheffield send up of its own habit is the phrase "Dont dee da me, dee da dissen and see how da likes it". A translation would be, "Don't you address me as thou, you address yourself as thou and see how you like it".

A Sheffield riddle is to translate the following:-

DEMS DONKEYS

RD

RDR

RDL
DR
ORDR
Translation: Them's donkeys. Are they. Aye, they are. Are they hell. They are. Oh aye, they are.

Dee da is still used by Barnsley football fans as a derogatory term for Sheffield Wednesday and United fans.

Diddle To cheat, "He's diddling thee"

Dinner When I was at school, dinner was always served in the middle of the day. Lunch, when the word was used at all, was a light meal or a sandwich. Nowadays the word is certainly used for the main meal, whatever time taken, but is also used by the middle classes for their evening meal. School pupils still refer to the people who work to provide their midday meals as 'dinner ladies'.

Diphthongs Sheffielders enjoy diphthongs and stretch them out and separate them whenever possible. Hence meat becomes `meeat`, door `dooer`. There are several examples in this glossary. In extreme cases it is even possible to manage a triphthong (if there is such a word).

Dipping In order to select the person who is `on` in such a game as tiggy or hide-and-seek dipping is necessary. Usually this involves some complicated procedure and/or rhymes to make the selection. The rhymes worked by the participants standing (usually) in a circle and being counted round, usually one person for each word, and dismissed in turn until only one was left. Sheffield children used a wide variety of these and some are as follows.

1. Each participant put both clenched fists out and the one conducting the dipping counted round the ring says, "One potato, two potato, three potato, four, five potato, six potato, seven potato, more" and the last fist counted on the word `more` is removed from the circle. This proceeds until only one fist is left and that person in `on`.

2. "Ickle ockle, chocolate bottle, ickle ockle out".

3. "Up a ladder, down a ladder in temptation, how many pigs went through the station? ..... One, two, three, little pigs went through the station, out goes you" The variation in this `dip` was that the counting went up and down the line, reversing each time the end was reached. At the place ..... the person pointed at chose a number (in this case 3) and the counting went from there. In theory at least it was possible to count up a number which would be to that person's advantage, I never saw anyone achieve this.

4. "Dip, dip, dip, my blue ship, sailing on the water, like a cup and saucer, dip, dip, dip, you are it."

These are just examples of a large number used.

Sometimes a rather sophisticated second chance was given to the selected person who was `on`. They stood with their back to the rest and the following was said. "I draw a snake on this man's back, who will end it with a tap". This was accompanied by the drawing of the snake and at the end of the rhyme one of the others would tap the end of the snake. If the person who was `on` guessed the right name, they changed places with that one and the game of tiggy, or whatever, started.

Dish clout Dish cloth.

Do Northern word for a party, celebration. "Tha should 'ave been at ahr Jack's weddin'. It wor a reight good do."

Dolled up Poshly dressed, probably from 'dolly', see below..

Dollop Large serving of food, mortar, cement, wallpaper paste, in fact anything which is semi liquid.

Dolly Polishing wheel.

Dolly posh is a Yorkshire dialect term for left handed. There was a conflict on new council estates in the 1930s onwards as people became mixed up and used different words for the same thing. In the difference regarding left handedness, cack handed seems to have won the argument in Sheffield.

Donkey stone Pieces of a soft, iron ochre-stained sandstone used to colour the edges of front steps. It must be thirty years at least since I saw a donkey stoned front step. Women, especially in the many terraced houses which had front doors opening straight on to the street, used donkey stone and chose their favourite colour and produced their own pattern of colouring, top edge only, top and sides, etc.

Dooer Pronunciation of door.

Doorways There is a common local superstition regarding the use of doorways. Many people will seek always to leave a building by the same door through which they entered. It is not long since a visitor to our house who entered by the back door, which had then been locked up, insisted on it being unlocked and opened so that they could leave the same way. The reasons for the superstition may be related to the concept of a guardian angel, waiting outside the building until their charge reappears; or it might be a vague belief in an `aura` around the person which cannot all pass into the doorway and so some is left outside to be collected on exiting. I suspect that most followers of the superstition have no idea why they do it, they are just following a family tradition.

I have heard that, for some, the tradition has it that if a different door is used and the person is female, this heralds the early arrival of a new baby.

Drove Driven. "'E 'as drove that car until it wor wore aht."

Drownded Drowned. There is a local tendency to double up the –ed ending (see berrited).

Dursn't Dare not. "Ah bet that tha dursn't go over theear an' ring t'vicar's dooer bell."

Earhole Ear. As likely to be 'earoil', meaning the same.

Elbow grease Hard manual work.

Else Used as preferable to `or else`. "Get thi 'omework done else tha'll 'ave no supper."

Emty Empty, the p is frequently omitted.

Entry The passage between two houses, usually with part of the houses built above it making a tunnel.

Etten Eaten. A preacher was conducting his first service at a village chapel and was invited to tea beforehand. He refused most of the food with the statement, "I am sorry, but I cannot preach well on a full stomach". After the service his host went up to him and said, "Tha may as well 'ave etten."

Ey up! A call for attention, "Ey up, sithee, there's a funeral." Sometimes used as a general greeting, "Ey up, lads".

Father Commonly pronounced to rhyme with `gather`, at least as a northerner would pronounce lather (with a short `a`).

Fauce Cheeky, but really more than cheeky, a sort of combination of cheeky, awkward and pretentious. I have not heard it for some time, but my mother (from Oughtibridge) used it in a semi joking way, usually as in "He's a right fauce hole". I have never seen it written so do not know how to spell it.

Favour To resemble, usually of a child, "She favours her mother".

Feight Fight. Hence the Sheffield school yard joke, "Wanna feight?" and the answer is "Seven" (work it out).

Fingers Sheffield has names for the fingers which are used to amuse small children:- (from the thumb) Harry Wible, Tommy Thible, Harry Whistle, Tommy Thistle, Little Uckabell.
The last is usually repeated as "Little Uckabelluckabelluckabelloo" accompanied by tickling the child.

Finger thumb and rusty bum Local name for a well known schoolyard game whereby two teams take it in turns to form a line of bent backs onto which the other team will leap and stay to hopefully cause the first to collapse.

Fishcake In Sheffield a fishcake is a sandwich of two slices from a large potato with a slice of fish in between, dipped in batter and fried, very healthy. What others call fishcakes are called rissoles in the city, as indeed we know they should be.

Flibberty gibbet A somewhat wilful and scatter-brained child, I have only heard it used of a girl.

Flipping... A euphemism for using a four letter swear word. It is common over the whole country, usually followed by heck, another euphemism, this time for hell. What seems only to be used in Sheffield is 'flipping early' with the 'ear' part sounding like those on the side of your head. "Flippin' early, tha's made me jump, comin' up be'ind me like that." Who or what 'early' is or was I have no idea.

Flit To move house. A local teacher, not native, was told by a girl, "I'm fli'in'". The girl became more and more exasperated at the failure to be understood and ended up shouting the phrase which the teacher only grasped when she asked a colleague later in the day what the girl meant.

Fogg (sometimes spelt `fog`). A rough grass, from the Danish. One species, called Yorkshire Fog, is probably the most beautiful of native wild grasses.

Fooil Fool. "`Ee were a reight fooil, allus getting' into a mess wi' lasses".

Four lane ends A cross roads. The top of Meadowhead was always called this until the roundabout was built and it was renamed. Many people still use the name for the area.

Frame To get along, particularly at work, as in, "How's thy new lad framin'?"

Fratchy Quarrelsome.

Freeten Frighten, also `freetened`, "Thart freetened on him".

French butterfly Any brightly coloured butterfly, red admiral and peacock in particular.

Fun Found (in the sense of discover), "Asta fun t' ball yet?"

Gaffer Boss, manager, owner of the company, locally also used for lesser mortals such as foreman, ganger etc.

Gallaces Braces - for trousers, not teeth.

Gammy leg Bad or injured leg which shows the injury, usually by a limp.

Ganister (various spellings) A sandstone with a very high silica content previously used for furnace linings, peculiar to the region.

Gansey A type of cardigan. From the island of Guernsey, just as Jerseys come from its neighbour.

Gate Road, from the Vikings. Many roads in the city centre bear the name `gate`, Fargate, Waingate, Castlegate and many newer ones such as Arundel, St. Mary's and Cutler's Gate. None refers to a gate in the sense of a barrier, the name for that would be `bar` as in West Bar, Owler Bar and Hunters Bar.

Gen Gave. "I gen 'im t' bus fare and 'e spent it on spice."

Gennell Alleyway. The `g` is soft, unlike further north in the county.

Gercher Get off, go away.

Get it This was the cry of the underdog when I was at school. When the class bully picked on a weaker boy, the cry from the sufferer would be, "Tha'll get it, thee," expressing a forlorn hope of some form of retribution.

Gi'o'er Give over. I had to include this in spite of my contention that slovenly speech is not dialect. It is the

widely used complaint of the Sheffield underdog, the
oppressed, the overworked, the tired.

Gob Mouth, also spit. Derivatives are `Gobby`
cannot keep a secret, and `gobbing` spitting.

Gobblety guts The leaves of wild sorrel which are
eatable with a somewhat sour, but not unpleasant,
taste. Can be eaten raw in salads or added to cooking.

Gollop Eat voraciously. "If tha keeps on golloping thi
food tha'll 'ave belly wark."

Goose pimples What the US citizens call `goose
bumps`.

Gormless Inane, silly. It strikes me that the dialect
has an inordinately large number of words for
silliness, few for intelligence. What does this say
about our predecessors?

Gradely Fit and well, or good, as in "How are tha?"
"Gradely".

Graft Work hard. "Ees a reight grafter."

Gumption Common sense.

H I have assumed that most of you will be aware that
the 'H' on all of the following words would almost

always be missing. This, of course, is not a Sheffield but a national trait. The only time you can count on the 'H' being sounded is, wrongly, on the name of the letter 'aitch', which of course has no 'H' anyway.

I believe that Sheffielders sincerely believe that they are pronouncing the `h`. Just listen to a native speaker when they are using a word or name without 'H' at the beginning, but which could perhaps have had one. They will pause, take a breath and pronounce the word with quite a lot of effort. "Our new minister's called Mester 'Unsworth." If the name had an 'H' it would be, "Our new minister's called Mestrunsworth."

Hagg Hump of peat on the moors, the ditches between are sometimes known as 'grikes'.

Half Was locally pronounced "Aif". There was an occasion, just prewar, when the captain of a local church football team read out the team in church. Eventually he arrived at, "Reight aif back, missen".

Half baked Rather simple minded (usually pronounced 'aif baked')

Happen Perhaps. "Happen ah'll come round to see thee t'neet".

Hen hoil Hen coop/run.

Hersen Herself. "When tha sees what daft things she does to 'ersen, she's 'er own worse enemy."

Hiddied Hidden. "Ah couldn't find our Mary anywheear, she wor 'iddied be'ind t'shed."

Hiding Flogging. "T' teacher gen 'im a reight hidin'"

Hissen Himself "T' silly beggar were sittin' in t' dark bi 'issen."

Hoil Hole

Hot aches Acute pains in (especially) the fingers, produced by too rapid warming of the hands after being very cold, such as by snowballing. I remember these excruciating pains and always vowed that it would never happen again, and it didn't (until the next time).

House place The living room, usually the kitchen, of a house. "Wheears t' mester?" "'Es in t' 'ouse place 'avin' 'is teea."

Howd Hold, the 'ow' part rhymes with 'cow'. "Cop howd of this hammer while I get t' nails".

Howd on To wait. "Howd on, ahm tryin' to catch up wi' thee."

Hull To shell peas

Hutch up A request to move along. Usually presented as a request to a person sitting on, for example, a bench. "Hutch up, ah want to sit dahn an' all, tha knows."

Jamb Door post

Joggle To rock or shake. You can joggle a key in a lock to make a person aware that you are at the door, you can joggle your loose tooth when you are about 6-7 years old.

k Frequently a –ing ending of a word is changed to –ink. One headteacher, who had been at college with me, would speak of 'teachink and learnink'.

Kecks Trousers

Kings Used to achieve a breathing space in a game, such as tiggy. Equivalent to `barley` or `parley` in some parts of the country.

Knock on To work faster. "We must knock on or else t' gaffer will wonder what we've been doing".

Knurr and spell A game (now extinct?) whereby a small billet of wood (the knurr) was placed across a thinner and longer piece in such a way that when the end of the first was hit hard by a mallet, or by a longer piece of wood, (the spell) it sprung into the air and the spell was then used to hit it as far as possible. Sophisticated ways of making the knurr leap into the air using springs were also used.

Lace To give a beating to.

Lads Any male, of any age. Workmates are `the lads`, schoolboys are also.

Laik (Variously spelt `laak`, `lake`) to play. Was used widely until some fifty or so years ago. It is of Danish origin and in Denmark provided the first part of the name of Lego, meaning `play good`.

Laik Monday Mondays were sometimes referred to as `Laik Monday` because of the widespread habit, especially in coal mining, of taking the day off as part of the weekend. Sometimes it was called `Saint Monday`. A leader of the NCB once addressed a meeting of miners and asked them why they only worked four days a week. The loud reply was "Because we can't bloody manage on three".

Laithe   Barn, usually remote from the main farmstead.

Lap To wrap. "She lapped babby in swadddlin' clooathes and laid 'im in a manger".

Lape To cover with, for example, jam. "He were laping t' jam on".

Larrap To cake with, especially, mud. `'E come 'ooam larraped wi' mud`.

Lasses Any female, workmates, schoolgirls, wife. "Our old lass has got hersen a new 'at".

Lat Lath

Learn Used both for `to learn` and `to teach` at random. "Ah'll learn thee who's t' boss 'ere if that comes that tone of voice wi' me ageean."

L

Leather To thrash. "If tha gives thi mother any mooer lip ah shall leather thee."

Leave go Release. "T' teacher were holding me arm and I asked him to leave go".

Leet Pronunciation of `light`. Sheffield joke; `I've got a four litre car, two leets at t' back and two at t' front'

Leg it Run away. "T' coppers is here, lets leg it".

Lend Borrow. "Can I lend thi ladder?" Beloved by Sheffield teachers down the ages because when a pupil asks "Can I lend a pencil" they can say "Who are you going to lend it to?" I was at a school where a boy came in and said "Can Mr Marshall lend your board compasses?" The teacher said "Of course he can't, I've got them." The triumphant pupil was able to say, "No, Sir! Mr Marshall has got your board compasses, he wants to lend them to Mr Shipley."

Lend can also mean a loan. "Gi'us a lend of thi 'ammer."

Lether staves A cut of ribs of beef. I have never seen it written, it could be also pronounced `ladder staves`.

Lick and a promise Meaning a washing of the face which was really of no consequence, usually applied in a hurry, just wiping the face over then drying it. "Ah told thee to wesh thi face and all tha's done is gi' it a lick an' a promise." Mothers often make brave attempts to give a lick and a promise to a child's dirty face with a hankerchief and some saliva.

Lief Rather. "I'd as lief go to t' pictures than t' dogs t'neet."

Lights Lungs and other offal used, after boiling, to feed cats or dogs.

Like There is a long history of this word being added to the end of Sheffield sentences, a habit now far more widespread. The word has no meaning whatsoever.

"I were goin' down t' rooad like and this fellow come up and asked me like wheear I were gooin'".

Lilly lo Child's talk (from an adult) meaning a light, such as a candle or an electric bulb.

Loise Lose. "Ah `spect Wednesday 'll loise ageean a Satdeh".

Lolloping Reference to clumsiness. A `lolloping great lump` was a clumsy person (usually male).

Loppy Dirty, from the Danish `Lop` a flea. Usually applied to people, "She were a loppy un".

Lopsided Not square or straight, applied to pictures, badly built walls etc.

Love Usual appellation in the district to anyone. Unlike most parts of Yorkshire, Sheffield people apply this as readily between members of the same sex as between different ones. A friend came to Sheffield from Huddersfield for an interview and asked the (male) bus driver for the cost of the fare. `Shilling, love` was the answer. My friend was just about to hit him when he realised that this was the local custom. Some offence has been taken to the use of the word by feminists, amongst others, it appears to have had little effect, thank goodness.

Lugs Ears (of people)

Lugs Matted knots in the hair which have to be combed out.

Manchester screwdriver Hammer. Used as a derogatory term for poor workmanship when a screw is hammered in rather than using a screwdriver. I understand that various such names are used all over the country, often with a reference to some local place. Perhaps somewhere there exists a `Sheffield screwdriver` (in Manchester even?).

Manking Messing around, usually with members of the opposite sex, eventually was almost wholly used in this context. "Whear 'as tha been? Asta been manking wi' them lasses ageean?" Or, even more cryptically, "Asta been mankin'?"

Manking dress I was delighted to learn from a woman who was born in Crookes that, when she was a girl, dresses with buttons down the front were known as `mankin' dresses`. I leave it to the more broad minded amongst you to work out why that was so. Personally, I have no idea.

Manky Anything that is bad or unsatisfactory can be manky. "I wor waitin' for t' bus an' it never came. It wor reight manky."

Mardy This Northern/Midlands word is widely used in Sheffield. It is descriptive of a sulky person, or one who too readily cries over trivial matters.

Mardy bum One who is mardy. "Tha'rt rooarin' agean. Thart a reight mardy bum. Ah've told thee, tha can't guh to t' pictures toneet."

Mash Southerners make tea with hot water, some Southerners brew their tea, Sheffielders, in common with most northerners, `mash` the tea.

Mashing A portion of tea large enough to be used to make a pot of tea.

Master Frequently pronounced with a short 'a'.

Mawngy Moth eaten (last time I heard it used was of a cat, so not literally moth eaten)

Mawngy Sulking. "When tha dunt get thi own way thart a reight mawngy beggar."

Me Frequently placed as an emphasis at the end of a sentence, really serves no useful purpose at all. "Ah've allus been a bit careful wi' brass, me."

Meh Pronunciation of me. "Ah asked t'mester for me ball back an' 'e gen it meh".

Mester Master, or mister. Used as a name for a man whose name is not known (eg. A child might say

"Please mester, have you got change for 10p"), also as a title, "Mester Brown". Children would stand outside the cinema on, particularly Saturday, evenings with the admission money in their hands asking to be taken into an A film with the request, "Please take us in, mester".

Self employed persons in the cutlery trade were known as "Little Mesters". These were often working in rented premises or even on a rented grinding wheel and bench in larger premises. In outlying villages they often worked in a small shed adjacent to their own homes. My wife's grandfather was the last little mester in Wadsley, making penknives. When her mother went to college and was asked the occupation of her father she said, "Little Mester, he makes cutlery" and it was listed as "Master Cutler".

Meyt Pronunciation of meat.

Middling Neither more nor less, applied to state of trade, state of health, weather etc. "Ow are tha feeling, Jack?" "Nobbut middling".

Mimmy moking Making facial expressions to pass on information to another, usually behind the back of a third party.

Mischief night Traditionally this was 30 April in Sheffield, but has moved relatively recently to 31

October in a sad imitation of the US custom of Hallowe'en. It was a time when young boys (mainly) unhinged gates, threw flour, tipped bins over etc.

Mizzling A weather condition somewhat worse than drizzling, usually cold, wet and misty.

Missen My self. "Me missen, I dooan't like cabbage".

Mither Sometimes pronounced 'Moither' meaning to bother. A mother might say to her child, "Stop mithering me".

Moan't Must not. Hard to write the pronunciation, it is nearly rhyming with won't (will not) but with the 'a' separated. "Tha moan't put thi feet on t' cushions else t' mester will get thee".

Moo cow Childish talk for cow.

Moonpenny Ox-eye daisies.

Moor cock Grouse (the bird).

Muck Dirt. Applies to dirt in the house, soil, rubbish, manure.

Nadden Now then, yet another example of the Sheffield tendancy to use `d` rather than `th`. This sometimes comes together as, "Nadden dee, wheear are da gooin?"

Naging (the `a` is long as in `day` and the `g` is hard as in `got`). Aggravating as (perhaps only) with a pain `a naging pain`.

Nah Now. Often used as a greeting, to which the response is to repeat, as in, "Nah, Tom." "Nah, Cecil."

Nah's come A man standing outside a pub heard the locks being undone at opening time and said to his mate, "Nah's come". The time we were waiting for has arrived.

Narked Annoyed

Near Tight with money. `He's a near one, nivver spends a penny`.

Neb Hard extension at the front of a cap.

Neb To poke ones nose in. 'Ah wor talkin' to our Sid an' your Jack wor nebbin' all t' time.'

Neet Night. Especially in the greeting, "'Neet, lad" meaning good night.

Neither nowt nor summat A matter of little importance. "'E wor goin' on ageean abaht ahr kid comin' in late, but ah told 'im it wor neither nowt not

47

summat."

Nesh Originally fearful, now most usually applied to those who are susceptible to feeling the cold. "Th'art nesh", for example. The original use was once shouted out at a Wednesday match when one of the home players avoided a tackle and a voice from the crowd shouted, "Tha's neshed it".

Nessy Lavatory. It derives from necessary, after all, the privy down the garden was probably the most necessary room of all. Its use probably comes from a 'polite' attempt never to actually refer to such places as lavatories.

Nevvy Nephew.

Nines As in `dressed to the nines` turned out in ones best clothes.

Nobbut Only, "He's nobbut just wed". From `nothing but`.

Nor Often used instead of `than`. "'E wor allus more clever nor any on us.'

Nowt Nothing (literally, `not owt`).

Of a Sunday (can be any day of the week, or indeed any time) On Sundays. "We gooa to see 'is Mam of a

Sunday, ivvery week." I have also heard, "We generally drink coffee of a morning and tea of an afternoon."

Off Can be used to mean `from` as in "I got it off my mate".

Off of As in "Get off of that wall" meaning `get down`.

Off on Alternative to `off of` or even to `off`. "I got it off on my mate". "Get off on that wall."

Off shot A part of a building which projects from the main part. Most commonly of the part at the back of many nineteenth century houses including the kitchen. This would be referred to as `an off-shot kitchen`.

Okker water The yellow water which flows from old iron workings, named after the iron ochre in the water.

Old stick Said affectionately of any older eccentric man. "`E`s a grand old stick, `e is.'

On Often used for `of` as in "He were one on 'em".

Once in a Sheffield Flood Meaning rarely. Was used certainly up to the 1960s, now has probably died out as the children of those who experienced the flood of 1864, following the Dale Dyke reservoir collapse have died.

I have been told that some people are still using this phrase.

Overlaid Got up late. This became the way of expressing lateness. It was very widely used from 1960s onwards. Since 'Overlaid' really refers to the placement of one item on the top of another, or to an excess production of eggs by a hen, it provided some simple amusement for the schoolteacher at the beginning of another busy day. The common response to the statement, 'Ah overlaid, sir (or 'miss')' was 'How many eggs was it today?' Since the pupil had not the foggiest idea what the teacher was talking about, the joke was very private (but satisfying, I must admit).

Owt Anything. (see `nowt`).

Panshion Large, usually pot, basin.

Pappy Soft, such as a 'pappy' apple.

Pey Pronunciation of `pea`.

Pie can Silly person. Used of the moment and meant humorously, "Tha piecan".

Pikelet Small oatcake.

Pike Peek. As, in a game of hide and seek, to the seeker who is counting whilst the rest are going to hide, "Stop piking".

Pleck A mucky house. "She lives in a right pleck".

Pobs Bread and milk as was fed to a child or invalid.

Poddy Baby talk for a shoe.

Poi Pronunciation of pie.

Poise To kick. "Get out of my yard or I'll poise thi arse".

Polly Child talk for head.

Polony From Bologna sausage. A local sausage containing finely milled sausage meat.

Poppo Was used as a child's name for a horse. I have not heard it for some years. It is supposed to be of Lincolnshire origin and came with ex farm workers from there seeking employment in the steel works.

Poss To press, or push. Especially remembered from the name for the implement used in a wash tub to press clothes, a 'posser' (or posher).

Posset Slight regurgitation of food from a milk fed baby. Can also be a verb, "T'babbie's posseted ageean."

Proud Sticking out. "When 'e 'd finished t' tilin' ah fun that 'ed left two on 'em proud and ah made 'im come back ageean."

Pubs Like many places, Sheffield has developed nicknames for many of its pubs. There is usually a slightly humorous use of these names and this has seduced some pub owners to change the name of the pub, somehow thinking that they can cash in on the humour. The result has been a sad loss of a local tradition as all sense of fun has been destroyed.

I give two examples. 'The Shakespeare' on Bradfield Road, Hillsborough, has been known affectionately as 'The Shakey' for years. It has survived the 1864 Sheffield Flood and two World Wars, but by renaming it 'The Shakey' the owners have demonstrated a lack of humour and destroyed the mateyness of the nickname.

The other is an even worse example. Just above Boots in Fargate there is a small lane named 'Black Swan Walk'. Here was 'The Black Swan', a pub with a long history and always known as 'The Mucky Duck' (the yard was also known as 'Mucky Duck Yard'). This was regarded as mild Sheffield humour. The name stuck, even when the pub was resited at the top of Snig Hill. By renaming the pub 'The Mucky Duck', the owners took away the fun and left us what was just a naff name. Perhaps that is why the pub was, sadly, renamed `The Boardwalk`.

Pun A pound, whether money or weight.

Puther An outpouring of smoke from (eg) a fire or a chimney.

Quart to Quarter to (of the time). One problem, or advantage, of living immersed in Sheffield dialect for a lifetime is that some of the words and phrases become normal speech and it was only recently, whilst making an appointment and told "Quart to twelve", that I realised that if this was not dialect, it would be "A quarter to twelve".

Race The outgoing channel from a water wheel, the mill race.

Rag Temper as in "Dooant loise thi rag".

Rake Strip of land.

Rammell General rubbish. Usually around a workplace.

Rammy Smelly.

Rare Very. `'E wor a rare good footballer in 'is day.`

Ratten To destroy tools, or to destroy a workplace. A rattener is one who does this. (Ratten was a very old dialect word for rat).Rattening was a common way of dealing with strike breakers and any others who threatened existing ways of life in the 19th century (especially) leading to the Sheffield atrocities whereby eventually gunpowder was used and led to terrible injuries and death. The gunpowder was placed in the grinding troughs so that when the workman sharpened his first blade of the day, the sparks would cause an explosion.

Rayther Rather. `Ahd rayther go to 'ell than go to watch United play`. (or Wednesday if you prefer).

Reight Pronunciation of right (rhymes with eight).

Rench Rinse.

Right Used as a description of something fairly extreme. "I went into t'stores for some bread an' there wor a reight queue."

Rooad Yet another widespread use of the Sheffield approach to a dipthong, if the sound is there, let someone hear it!

Rooar To cry, as babies do. "Stop thi rooaring".

Rosin Resin (trade term).

Rowan See Mountain Ash.

Rubbage Rubbish.

Ruffle topping With uncontrollable hair. "He's a little ruffle topping."

Sad As of a cake or loaf which has collapsed due to undercooking.

Saint Monday Any Monday, used to describe the widespread practice of using Monday to extend the weekend by not working on it. (See `laik Monday`).

Salary Celery.

Salt box A salt box was a wooden box, usually hanging on the kitchen wall, with a single, sloping, hinged lid. Because of the similar shape, any building erected with a roof that shape was known as a salt box house`. This is the origin of Salt Box Lane at Grenoside.

Sam To get hold of, or to pick up. On being offered the handle of a spade, "Sam 'od on it", or on seeing a dropped tool, "Sam yon file up".

Scods Pea pods.

Scoil Pronunciation of school.

R
S

Scone Pronounced to rhyme with `tone` unlike many parts of the country where it rhymes with `gone`.

Scotch Piece of wood used to stop carts running backwards (also see 'chock').

Screw Pay (as a noun, for work done). "Ah get mi screw a Friday at t' end o' day".

Scroam To scramble about, I have heard it used most often to describe the clambering of children over their parents or grandparents. "He's allus scroaming about on me".

Scromping When I was a boy, all fruit growing in the open was considered a legitimate target, we obtained apples, pears and rhubarb. We hid the theft aspect of these activities by calling it scromping, but really it was theft, perhaps that is why it seemed to taste so good, even the rhubarb.

Scropadiddle Affectionate name for an active and inquisitive child. I last heard this used last week, my wife uses it for our grandchildren.

Seea An emphatic form of `see`, used to draw attention. "Nah seea" means look carefully at what I am about to show you. Can also be used as a warning in an argument, meaning, `look out`, or 'behave yourself'. A parent might say, to an unruly child,

"Nah seea, I shall clock thi one in a minute."

Seet Pronunciation of sight.

Sempt Seemed. "When she come in it sempt as though she wor sleepwalkin'."

Sen Self, as in `misen` (myself), `hissen` (himself) etc.

Sermons The popular name for Sunday School Anniversaries. These were massive affairs, often having little to do with the children. A stepped platform was erected on which the children sat, a massed choir of both local and visiting singers was assembled, often with an orchestra of invited players. Many members of the choir and orchestra went on a late spring/summer tour of the various chapels and sang or played at anniversary after anniversary as a sort of troupe of travelling players.

Set pot This was the large iron pot placed, usually, between the kitchen sink and the kitchen range. It had its own separate fire underneath and was filled with water which was heated to be used for clothes washing. Was also used for bathing small children.

Setts Cobblestones.

Shak Pronunciation of `shake`.

Shant (pronounced to rhyme with rant) I have only heard this word used in the sense of `all over the shant`, meaning all over the place. "When I got 'ooam there were watter all o'er t'shant 'cos we 'ad a brussen pipe ageean".

Shift To provide for oneself, or get a move on. "Tha'll have to shift for thissen".

Shoon Plural of shoes. Uses the same Old English ending as oxen or children.

Shortarse a small person. I heard a young boy saying to his companion, "I'm just like me dad, I'm a shortarse as well".

Shortening Lard.

Shove over Move up.

Shunkle To shine, sparkle or glitter. Probably more frequently met as 'shunkly', shiny. Can be applied to jewellery, Christmas decorations, frosty nights, Christmas cards with frost on them, stars, anything. "Did tha see our mam last neet in 'er new jewellery? It war all shunkly in t' candle leet."

Shut of Get shut of is to get rid of. A woman whose wayward husband has been sent packing said, "Wey, I've just got shut of him". Often used as 'Shut on'.

Side To clear, particular the pots and cutlery on a table, that is to put them on the side. "Tha can get off on thi backside and 'elp me to side t' pots."

Sile Pour (with rain). "It were siling down". This comes from the Danish word for a sieve, the rain is as heavy as water pouring through a sieve. If you have ever been out when it has been siling down, you will understand.

Sin Since. `I've been waitin' 'ere sin hafe past four`.

Skerrick Scrap. Eg. if all the food has been eaten, "There weren't a skerrick left".

Skinny Mean, a person mean with money is a `skinny beggar`.

Slack Poor quality coal.

Slake To wash down with a brush, to dampen down the dust on the floor.

S

Slape Lay on thickly. "She were slaping butter on like it cost nowt".

Slive To sneak. "Ahr kid slived a biscuit off of me mam's palte." "T'gaffer caught ahr Fred slivin' past t' clock machine an' sacked 'im."

Sloam Creep, as in "He were sloaming all over t' boss aggean"

Slobber Slaver, drool.

Smithereens To smash into smithereens, to break into small pieces (usually of pottery).

Smittle To be attracted to. "She were smittled with him".

Smittle Infected by. `Ahr kid wor smittled wi' t' measles'.

Snake thi cale To frustrate some other person in an activity. Thus, if one person's intention is to sit on a particular seat and another beats them to it, the second might say, "Ah snaked 'is cale". The old dialect lists give `cale` as meaning to take turns, but I have only heard it used as shown. I would guess that `snake` is a mispronunciation of `sneak`, so that the phrase would then mean `sneaked your turn`.

Snap Food taken to work for eating in the middle of the shift.

Sneck The latch on a door, by extension this has also been applied to a large nose with a pronounced bend in it. A police superintendent on duty frequently at

Hillsborough was alway known as `Sneck` by the crowd. A gift to take home for 'the wife' is still sometimes called a 'sneck lifter', in other words it can be used to deter wrath at a late home coming as soon as one enters the house, or even as a bribe to be let in if the door has been bolted.

Snig (As in Snig Hill) either the scotches used to prevent a cart running backwards down a steep road or the act of using such scotches.

Snitch Tell tales, also used as a noun, a tale teller.

Snitch Nose

Sooner Rather. "I'd sooner dee than gooa to live in Lancashire".

Sough A drain, usually from a mine working pronounced 'suff'.

Souse Soak

S

Spelch Used when a surface begins to shed material, could be by weathering (such as a brick or concrete) or by heating (as a metal block) or any other cause.

Spell A piece of thin wood or a roll of paper used to get a light from a candle or from the fire. Also used of a sliver of wood penetrating the skin.

Spice Sweets, Sheffield children buy sweets at a spice shop.

Spice cake Fruit cake.

Spozzy Lucky. A friend described his wife (a good card player) as `spozzy sod` whenever she won. Just recently a plumber managed a difficult manoeuvre in a tight place. I congratulated him on it, he said "Spozzy".

Starved Cold. "Ah were fair starved at t' match today". This is a common Yorkshire use of the word, but I have only once heard the equally common Yorkshire word `clemmed` used for `hungry` in Sheffield.

Steading A farm.

Stonks At the end of the second world war there was a shortage of almost everything. Glass marble manufacture was not a priority and for a fair time only pot marbles were obtainable as new. These were derided as `stonks` and their value was much smaller than the pre-war glass superior types. I seem to remember that the exchange rate was as high as five stonks for a glass marble.

Stooan Pronunciation of `stone`.

Stoop A post at the side of the road or a gatepost.

Stoothing Pronunciation of `studding` as in a wall built with timber framing.

Stores The Cooperative stores. "Ahm gooin' to t'stooers for some bacon." Was used far more often than 'Coop'. There used to be a number of societies in the area, Oughtibridge, Stocksbridge, Woodhouse and Chapeltown I remember as having their own societies. The major ones in the city were Sheffield & Ecclesall, and Brightside & Carbrook. The former was regarded as the posher, being mainly in the South and West, the latter was by far the larger and it is this one which transformed into the modern Sheffield Coop and has now been absorbed into the national chain.

Summat Something.

Sup Drink. "Dost tha want a sup before tha goes out?"

Supper A snack taken late in the evening before going to bed, not a main meal.

Swig A drink, usually no more than a mouthful.

Syke A ditch.

T' (My way of writing it). The Northern, especially Yorkshire, pronunciation of `the`. Southern ears

63

often fail to hear the t' which is a glottal stop, not a total dropping of the word, in fact most northerners are unaware of what they are doing. (Many teenagers of today use the glottal stop in such words as `butter` where they drop the `tt` and replace it with a glottal stop - `bu'er`.) I had a teacher on the same staff as me who consistently got into trouble for dropping `the` from speech. He was adamant that this was not what he did. After hearing him speak it was obvious that he used the glottal stop, and was convinced that in using it he was actually saying `the`. The difference can be seen in the phrases `In-house` and `In t' house`. To say the second properly requires a definite break in the throat which is audible. A common `Sheffield` saying is, 'Asta been dahn Twicker weear Twatter runs o'er Tweir'. This is fake Shefield dialect, a proper Sheffielder would never, never say, 'I'm going down Twicker', but would say, 'I'm going down t' Wicker'. (Similarly with t'watter and t'weir.)

The line, `Then t'worms 'll come an' eight thee up` from "Ilkley Moor" is also usually wrongly presented with tworms being sung as one word, especially by southerners.

T

Tacher   Sometimes used as pronunciation of `teacher`.

Tally man   A man (usually) who provided clothing or, less frequently, other needed items on credit. These were paid for on a weekly basis by the tally man going door to door. His profit was in the credit charges as well as the fact that he bought wholesale.

Tases Tastes. Pronunciation is as `tasers` but with a soft `s` in the middle.

Tay Tea, the drink.

Tea A meal taken after returning from work or school. Although it could be substantial, it would never be called dinner, that being reserved for a meal taken in the middle of the day. Again the diphthong is frequently sounded in full as `teea`.

Teem Pour.

Teeming and lading Balancing a rather dodgy balance by moving bits from one side to another. Could be money, but not necessarily so. "He's teemin' and ladin', tryin' to balance t' books"

Teeny Tiny

Tegs Teeth (in the mouth), usually restricted to addressing a toddler.

Telled Told. "I telled im as how he were late."

Tenses Present tense particular is used at random to mean any time. "We come 'ooam an' me mam'd not got teea ready an' me dad gets all ratty ageean."

Tenter One who attends to such as an engine, or any piece of machinery. An engine tenter.

Tew To work hard, 'to tew and toil'.

Tha Second person singular `you`. From `thou` which is archaic in accepted speech, but `tha` is far from archaic in Sheffield. "Tha daft fooil". Like many Sheffield children I grew up bilingual with standard Northern English at home and school and Sheffield in the playground. Just a few years ago I was on Penistone Road when a lorry driver stopped and said, "Hey up, dosta know wheear Easterbrook Allcard's is?" I heard myself say, "Aye, tha sees yon red leet….". My mother would have killed me.

Tha'd literally, `Thou would`.

Thart Thou art, i.e. You are. "Thart soft in t' 'eead to be wastin' thi time watchin' United." (or Wednesday if you prefer).

Thee `You` as in the emphatic sense. "Thee! Tha couldn't knock t' skin off of a rice pudden".

Theer There

Theirsens Themselves.

Them Frequently used instead of `those`. "Get over theear an' pick up them boooks an' bring 'em 'ere."

Thick Close. As with friends or conspirators.

Things happen in threes I suspect that this is a more widespread superstition than just Sheffield. The idea is that bad things happen in threes. I have known many people who believe this. Several of them would count `tragedies` in threes such as, one, banging head, two, dropping cup, then they would take a match and snap it as the third event to stop the series.

They were quite right, of course, things do happen in threes, so long as you start counting again as soon as three is reached. They also happen in fours, in hundreds and in millions, or any other in number that you chose to count in.

Thingy The local choice for what in many places will be 'whatchamacallit', or 'whatsitsname'. Used often to be pronounced 'fingy' Can produce some extremely obscure sentences. "Ah put t' fingy on t' fingy and t' mester said to move it."

T

Throng Crowded. "I came 'ome from t' market cos it were so throng'

Tib and Lal A reference to a close friendship between two females, not sexual. "They're just like Tib and Lal." I have no idea of the origin, I suppose they were well known characters at some distant time in the past.

Tiggy A game of tag, also called 'tig'.

Tingerlary Used as a word for a barrel organ (which I have never heard) and also somewhat disparagingly to an ice cream van with its chimes.

Tipple To topple.

Tippy toes Tip toes.

Tittivate To prepare oneself in finery for going out. "She's upstairs tittivating hersen aggeean".

Tooa Pronunciation of toe.

Tossing ring These were gambling schools that met in various parts of the city. The most famous met on Sky Edge. The `tosser` held his hand out, palm upwards with three halfpennies on the ends of his fingers. He then flung them into the air and bets were laid on the numbers of heads or tails displayed on landing on the ground. Gangs took over the rings in the early part of the last century and fought each other for control of various rings. The ensuing gang wars made Sheffield notorious. The amounts of money were great, police were corrupted and murder took place. A new Chief Constable and a policy of only employing police who had no family connections to the city ended the practice. That is how my father, a Darton man, came to join the police and live in Sheffield in the early 1930s. Never the less, the last tossing ring was still operating until the 1950s at `The Magnet` at Southey Green.

Touch burner (could be torch burner?) In the north of the city, this is the name for what in the south is called a winter warmer. It was made, usually by boys, from clay. It comprised an open topped box with holes in the side. In the box was placed pieces of cloth which were set alight and allowed to smoulder. By blowing through the holes, or allowing the wind to do so, the cloth would burn brighter and smokier. The device became quite hot. A more effective way of raising the temperature was to suspend the whole from string passed through the holes and whirl it in the air. There was always a danger that the string would burn through and the box fall and break, in fact, when being whirled at speed, there was a great danger that an onlooker would get an eye full of very hot clay!

Tracle Treacle.

Trankliments I have never seen it spelled so have written it as said. It refers to any complicated device or any which seems strange or even personal clutter. So it could be said of a man carrying a new machine, "Look at our Joe, what's that trankliment he's

T

carrying?", or of a workshop, "I've nivver seen such a collection of trankliments in my life".

Trazz To travel fast, often rather recklessly. I thought that this was really a 1940s schoolboy slang word and had died out, but I have heard it used twice, by different people, in the past few weeks. " We went aht on us bikes to t'top o' City Rooad and when we came back dahn Granville Rooad we weren't aif trazzin'"

Tret Common pronunciation of `treat`. "Ah tret missen to a new 'at."

Tuffet Is used as an alternative to `buffet` meaning a `pouffee`. I certainly have heard this as recently as 2006.

Tup A ram.

Upend Turn upside down.

Upsidaisy Comment when some minor accident has occurred.

Us Used for `our` or for `me` as well as for `us`. Generally pronounced `Uzz` with a hard `u`. (Oddly enough this pronunciation is never used for `bus` as it is in Manchester, in Sheffield the ending is always `ss`.) The variety of uses give such as a common request when I was at primary school and eating an apple, "Gi'us thi cowk", "Teacher came into us lesson and telled us off", "Miss says we've got to get us 'ymnbooks".

Wagon A lorry.

Waint Contraction of `will not`. "He waint put his shoes on, Mam."

Wak Wake as in awaken. Also `wakken up`, waken up. "Tha wants to waken thi ideas up, tha'll nivver get nowheear actin' like tha does."

Wants Sometimes used to describe the time before and event. A Wadsley man, a teetotaller, was passing the `Star` (now the `Wadsley Jack`) and a man waiting for opening time asked him what time it was. "It wants ten minutes", was the answer.

War Was. "He war a reight mardy bugger when he were a babby".

Wark Ache. I have heard it as `belly wark`, `Ead (head) wark` and `ear wark`.

Warm Well off, "He's a warm 'un".

Was Used also for `were`. "Was you at the match last neet?" See also `were` for the opposite effect.

Watter Pronunciation of `water`.

Way Well. "Way, ah dooant know wheear she can be, she wor 'ere just a minute aguh."

Weeny Small.

Were Used for `was`, "I were late for work because our lass were badly".

Werrited Worried, using an extra syllable as in 'Berrited'.

Wesh Pronunciation of wash. "Get into yon kitchen an' wesh thi 'ands, tha mucky little tooad."

Whacking Big, very big.

What Often put into a sentence as an emphatic addition which would not be present in Standard English. A recent television interview with a local had the following sentence, "They are a lot worse off than what we are".

Wheear Pronunciation of `where`. Has had a strange effect on some inhabitants who aspire to raising their station in life. Knowing that `wheear` is wrong for `where`, they expand on this and decide that it might also be wrong for `weir`, of which there are many in Sheffield, so they pronounce that word also as `where`. They end up sounding just what they are, pretentious.

When ness When necessary. Getting 22 players for a game of football was almost always impossible. Therefore the `goalie when necessary` was invented, a player who was a goalkeeper when one was needed, but a free agent at other times. This was the `goalie when ness`, pronounced in a variety of ways. Where I played the pronunciation was usually, `wegnest`.

While Means `until`. "I'm away on me holidays from Monday while Friday". This is a common usage in Yorkshire and it is claimed that a North Yorkshire Councillor waited at a railway automatic barrier which instructed `Wait here while the red light is flashing` and set off when the light flashed, escaping by a narrow margin. I heard a woman in the Northern General in 2006 say, "I shall have to wait while somebody comes to fetch me".

Wickets When playing street cricket, it was unusual to have two batsman in at the same time (even more unusual to have two bats), therefore the single one had to run one way and walk back for a single run. To make it clear that the running had finished at the bowler's end, the batsman would shout `wickets` when the first run was completed.

Winter hedge Clothes horse. People originally dried

clothes by spreading them over the nearby hedgerow. In winter this was not practicable so they hung them inside over the `Winter `edge`.

Winter warmer See touch burner.

Wood in the hole If the door is left open, the call will come "Put t' wood in t' oil", or `close the door`.

Wore Worn. "Ah 'ad to get 'er a new pair o' shoes cos 'er old ones were wore aht".

Wreckling The runt of the litter.

Wun To be wound. "Ah've wun t' clock up, love."

-y: The –y ending on words in invariably pronounced with a sound like `eh` by those with a true Sheffield accent. They are quite unaware of this and making a change is extremely difficult. I heard a senior manager in a local company recently referring to "Saturdeh" and "suddenleh", etc all through his speech.

Young Sometimes used to indicate sonship. A friend of my father's (my father's name was Frank) frequently referred to me as `young Frank`. I suppose it saved having to learn new names.

Young 'un Referring to a younger sibling, usually a

boy. "I can't come aht wi' thee today. I've got to look after our young 'un."

Yourn Yours, using the –n ending as found in mine and thine.

There you have it, I am not aware of any words beginning with 'z' which might have been a more fitting ending, but I have tried to present a fast dying tradition. It is relatively easy to preserve such as The Wicker Arches and Manor Lodge, it is probably impossible to preserve patterns of speech. Sheffield dialect is dying, not totally, but many of the words in this list have already dropped out of everyday speech, others will follow soon. I hope you have enjoyed what for some will be a nostalgic trip down memory lane and for others will probably be a revelation.

Printed in Poland
by Amazon Fulfillment
Poland Sp. z o.o., Wrocław